VOLCANOES & EARTHQUAKES

VOLCANOES & EARTHQUAKES

Monalisa Sengupta

PowerKiDS
press

New York

Published in 2008 by The Rosen Publishing Group, Inc.
29 East 21st Street, New York, NY 10010

First Published: 2005
Designed by Q2A Media

Picture credits:
t=top b=bottom m=middle l=left r=right c=centre
U.S. Geological Survey (USGS): 11bl, 21tl, 25m, 28bl, 29t, 30m, 31tl, 31b, 33l, 33m, 34bl, 34m, 38b, 43tl
D.A. Swanson/U.S. Geological Survey (USGS): 7t
R.L. Christiansen/U.S. Geological Survey (USGS): 9tm, 23br
C. Stoughton/U.S. Geological Survey (USGS): 10tr
J.D. Griggs/D.A. Swanson/U.S. Geological Survey (USGS): 21m
D.W. Peterson/U.S. Geological Survey (USGS): 23m
R.L. Christiansen/J.D. Griggs/U.S. Geological Survey (USGS): 25br
J.D. Griggs/U.S. Geological Survey (USGS): 24bl
Austin Post/U.S. Geological Survey (USGS): 26tr
D.W. Peterson/R.L. Christiansen/U.S. Geological Survey (USGS): 26bl
R.T. Holcomb/D.A. Swanson/U.S. Geological Survey (USGS): 42bl
Office of Oceanic and Atmospheric Research (OAR)/National Undersea Research Program (NURP): 12tr, 14bl, 24tr
National Aeronautics and Space Administration (NASA): 18tr, 19t, 19b, 42br
Commander John Bortniak/
National Oceanic and Atmospheric Administration (NOAA): 13m
Digital Globe: 35t, 35br

Library of Congress Cataloging-in-Publication Data

Sengupta, Monalisa.
  Volcanoes and earthquakes / Monalisa Sengupta.
    p. cm. — (Wild nature)
  Includes bibliographical references and index.
  ISBN-13: 978-1-4042-3901-2 (library binding)
  ISBN-10: 1-4042-3901-4 (library binding)
  1. Volcanoes—Juvenile literature. 2. Earthquakes—Juvenile literature. I. Title.
  QE521.3.S458 2008
  551.2—dc22

                    2007008688

Manufactured in China

C O N T E N T S

Inside the Earth

The ground under your feet may feel all strong and firm, but the Earth's inside is far from that. The topmost covering of the Earth is called the crust. The crust has three layers under it: the mantle, the outer core and the inner core. The crust and the upper mantle make up the lithosphere.

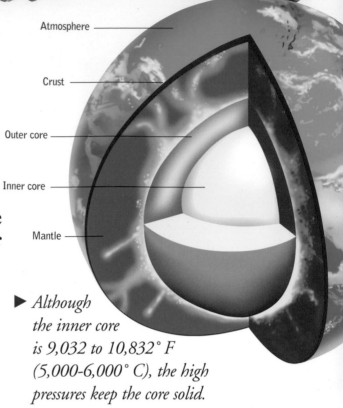

Atmosphere

Crust

Outer core

Inner core

Mantle

▶ *Although the inner core is 9,032 to 10,832° F (5,000-6,000° C), the high pressures keep the core solid.*

Hot as the Sun

The mantle is a thick layer of rock below the crust and is made up of silicon, oxygen, aluminum, iron and magnesium. Next comes the outer core, which is in molten liquid form. At the center of the Earth is the inner core and it is believed to be as hot as the Sun!

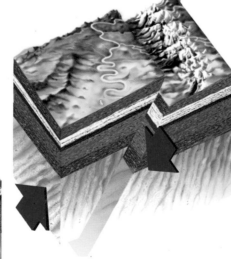

▼ *As the tectonic plates on the Earth's crust move, they often hit each other at the edges. Here the plates are sliding past each other.*

▲ *When tectonic plates strike against each other, one plate usually pushes under the other one.*

Like a football

Just as a football has many joints on its surface, the Earth's crust is also made of rocky plates placed next to each other. These are called tectonic plates. Unlike a football though, these plates are not joined and often collide with each other.

Getting shaky

Most earthquakes occur along the boundaries of the rocky plates. These plates collide against each other, causing the Earth to shake—either mildly or really hard!

Throwing up fire

When the Earth spews out melted rock from deep within, it leads to volcanoes. Volcanoes are openings on the Earth's surface through which lava, hot gases and rock fragments erupt.

▲ *Volcanic eruptions throw up three kinds of materials: lava, rocks and gases.*

Coastal plain

Shoreline

Mid-ocean ridge

Ocean

Shelf

Slope

Rise

Submarine canyon

Deep sea

Rising magma

▲ *Plates on the Earth's lithosphere can be less than 5 miles (8 km) thick beneath the ocean floors, or as much as 124 miles (200 km) thick under the continents.*

Volcanoes

An erupting volcano is perhaps one of the most spectacular sights on Earth. Volcanoes are like nature's own fireworks, but these are much more powerful and dangerous. A violent eruption can blow apart an entire mountain.

▶ *Most volcanoes erupt with enormous force, throwing lava, fireballs and ash high into the air.*

Awesome power

Powerful activities within the Earth cause volcanoes. An opening on the Earth's surface is formed, through which lava, hot gases and rock fragments spew out.

Ash and smoke

Central vent

Magma

Conduit

Melting magma

Extreme heat inside the Earth melts the rocks to form magma and gas. The gas-filled magma slowly rises toward the Earth's surface from the mantle. As more magma rises, it forms a large chamber near to the surface.

Chamber

◀ *The volcanic materials gradually pile up around the vent, forming a volcanic mountain, or volcano.*

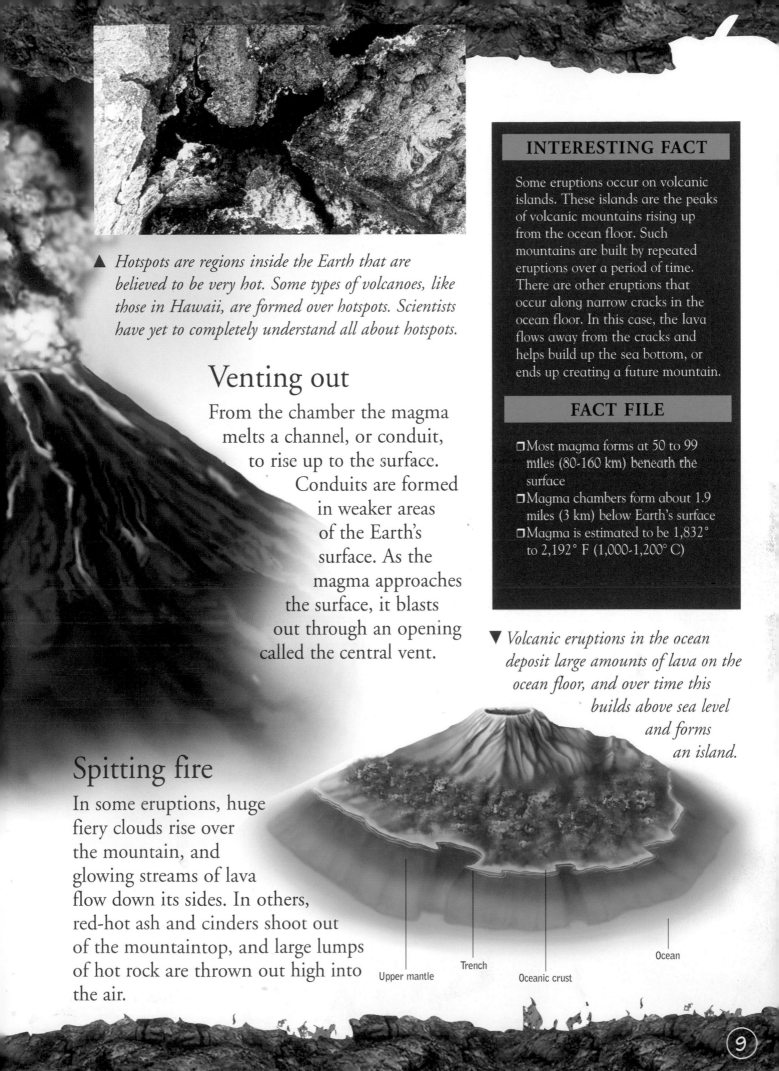

▲ *Hotspots are regions inside the Earth that are believed to be very hot. Some types of volcanoes, like those in Hawaii, are formed over hotspots. Scientists have yet to completely understand all about hotspots.*

Venting out

From the chamber the magma melts a channel, or conduit, to rise up to the surface. Conduits are formed in weaker areas of the Earth's surface. As the magma approaches the surface, it blasts out through an opening called the central vent.

▼ *Volcanic eruptions in the ocean deposit large amounts of lava on the ocean floor, and over time this builds above sea level and forms an island.*

Spitting fire

In some eruptions, huge fiery clouds rise over the mountain, and glowing streams of lava flow down its sides. In others, red-hot ash and cinders shoot out of the mountaintop, and large lumps of hot rock are thrown out high into the air.

Upper mantle

Trench

Oceanic crust

Ocean

Volcano Classification

Not all volcanoes are alike and scientists divide them in many ways, depending on how often they erupt, their shape, the kind of molten rock they are made of, and more.

On and off

Active volcanoes are those that either erupt constantly or have erupted in recent times. Although generally quiet, they can be violent at times. Intermittent volcanoes erupt at regular periods, while dormant volcanoes are the sleeping ones—they have become inactive for a while, but an eruption is possible again. Extinct volcanoes have been inactive during recorded history. They probably will never erupt again.

▲ *Lava eruption at Kilauea Iki, a crater situated east of the active Kilauea volcano in Hawaii.*

◄ *Mt. Kilimanjaro is a dormant, snow-capped volcano. Located in Tanzania, it is the highest mountain in Africa.*

Free-flowing

Shield volcanoes are formed when a large amount of free-flowing lava spills from a vent and spreads widely. The lava slowly builds up a low, broad and dome-shaped mountain. Thousands of separate, overlapping lava streams, each less than 49 feet (15 m) thick, formed Mauna Loa in Hawaii.

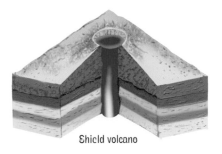
Shield volcano

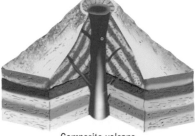
Composite volcano

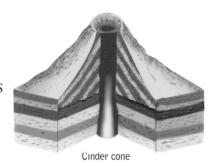
Cinder cone

▲ *Among the prominent types of volcanic landforms are shield volcanoes, cinder cones and composite volcanoes.*

Layered on

Composite volcanoes are formed when both lava and rock fragments erupt from a central vent. These materials pile up in alternate layers around the vent. Several such layers build up into a towering, and usually cone-shaped, mountain.

◄ *A feature of the Lassen Volcanic National Park, at the Cascade Range in northern California, is the Lassen volcanic peak. The volcano erupted last in 1921.*

Conically inclined

Cinder cones build up when mostly rocky material erupts and falls back to gather around the vent. The accumulated material, mostly cinders, forms a cone-shaped mountain with a bowl-shaped crater at the top. The height can vary from a few feet (m) to several hundred feet (m).

Volcanoes Under Sea

Most volcanic eruptions occur on ocean floors. These submarine eruptions occur along narrow cracks in the ocean floor. The lava flows away from the cracks, building up the sea bottom or the sea crust. However, nobody has yet observed a deep submarine eruption live.

Invisible

Since most submarine eruptions occur in the deep, one cannot see them from the surface. Only special features formed by the volcanic action have been observed. Submarine volcanoes can lead to island formation, as the erupted lava and volcanic matter accumulate over the years.

▲ *Pillow lava is formed when molten rock comes in contact with cold water or when eruptions occur in the sea.*

Cool and solid

The high pressure exerted by the water makes oceanic volcanoes behave differently from the ones situated on land. The pressure keeps the gases and steam in solution, preventing any violent explosion. Usually, the lava flows down the slopes slowly in long "pillow" shapes. The lava cools down quickly to become solid, and tends to collect along the sides of the slope.

Trench
Spreading ridge
Oceanic plate
Upper mantle
Magma chamber
Lower mantle
Molten core

◄ *The mid-ocean ridge system encircles the Earth like the seams of a baseball. The Earth's crust on these seams is continually moving apart, creating new ocean floor. The ridges have thousands of individual volcanoes that erupt periodically.*

Sand and rubble

Lava erupting from volcanoes on a shallow sea floor, or flowing into the sea from land, cools very rapidly. This splits the lava into sand and rubble, which may get deposited on the coastal areas, as in the case of the famous "black sand" beaches of Hawaii.

▼ *The black sand beaches of Hawaii were created by the violent interaction between hot lava and seawater.*

◄ *Chimney-like structures called "black smokers" form when hot water flows out through volcanic lava on a mid-ocean ridge.*

► *Tubeworms, some up to 5 feet (1.5 m) long, cluster around hot springs on the ocean floor.*

Shallow waters

When volcanoes erupt in shallow waters, they can blast steam and rock debris high above the sea surface. The ocean currents can cause the debris to drift over a large area. Most debris usually gets deposited on the sea floor, though.

Rocks and Minerals

▼ *The violet-colored amethyst is a form of the mineral quartz and is prized as a gem.*

Three kinds of materials can erupt from a volcano. These include lava, rock fragments and gas. The material that comes out of volcanoes depends chiefly on how sticky or fluid the magma is.

Red-hot

Lava is the name for magma that has escaped on to the Earth's surface. When lava reaches the surface, it is extremely hot. Then, as it starts to cool down, the lava hardens into different kinds of matter.

Rocky matter

Igneous rocks such as basalt are formed as lava cools above the ground. Such rocks are also created when the magma gets trapped in small pockets inside the Earth. These cool off slowly to form igneous rocks like granite.

◄ *The ocean floor is mostly made up of basalt, which is formed by lava flowing from cracks in the mid-ocean ridge.*

Mineral mine

Most of the metallic minerals mined in the world, such as copper, gold, silver, lead and zinc, are a result of volcanic activities over the years. These minerals are found in magma deep in the roots of extinct volcanoes, and are mined from there.

FACT FILE

- **Lava temperature:** More than 2,012° F (1,100° C)
- **Volcanic dust:** Diameter less than .01 inch (.25 mm)
- **Volcanic ash:** Diameter less than .2 inch (.5 cm)
- **Volcanic bomb:** Diameter over 2.5 inches (64 mm)

◄ *Diamonds are brought to the surface from the mantle in an unusual type of magma called kimberlite, which erupts at a type of volcanic vent called a diatreme or pipe.*

▼ *Pumice rocks are igneous rocks formed when the lava cools quickly above the ground. The rocks are very light and have pores on them.*

Blasting tephra

Rock fragments called tephra originate in sticky magma. Since the magma is sticky, it does not allow the gas to escape. The trapped gas builds up so much pressure that it blasts the magma into fragments. Tephra includes volcanic dust, volcanic ash and volcanic bombs.

Geysers and Hot Springs

Apart from erupting vents, the areas around volcanoes have other interesting features as well. These include hot springs and water geysers. Mud pots are formed when the heated water is mixed with mud and clay over the vent. The gases trying to escape through the vent causes the mud pot to bubble. If the hot water reaches the surface only in the form of steam, it is called a fumarole.

▲ *The water in hot springs often boils to give off steam. One can even see bubbles on the surface. The Crested Pool at Yellowstone National Park is one such hot spring.*

▼ *People believe minerals in hot springs are helpful for health. Many take baths in them to treat rheumatism and other ailments.*

Hot springs

Hot springs are gushes of hot water that are found on the land surface. These are formed when molten materials deep in the Earth cool down, giving off water vapor. The hot vapor moves up through cracks in the rocks, cooling down in the process. Gradually it condenses to become water and pours forth from the ground.

▶ *Geysers usually discharge hot water and steam up to heights of 164 feet (50 m).*

Rich in mineral

The water from hot springs is clear and rich in mineral content. The minerals are dissolved from the rocks as these move from under the Earth. Countries such as Japan, New Zealand, Kenya and Iceland are well-known for hot springs.

Natural fountains

Geysers are nature's own fountains of water wherein a vent at the surface throws up jets of hot water and steam. Scientists believe these are created when water enters cavities inside the Earth's surface and interacts with rock heated by magma.

Shooting up

The heat from the molten rocks boils the water and the high pressure builds up bubbles of steam. Finally, the pressure is strong enough to shoot out the water and steam upwards through a vent. This cycle can be repeated regularly.

◀ *Fumaroles are weak geysers that vent out volcanic gases, such as sulphur vapor, from fissures.*

Extraterrestrial Volcanoes

Earth is not the only place where volcanoes occur. Scientists have observed proof of volcanic activities on the Earth's Moon and other planets of the solar system. Volcanoes on the Moon and planets such as Mars and Venus are nearly three to four billion years old.

Sea of lava

The Earth's Moon has no large volcanoes like the Hawaiian ones or Mount St. Helens in the United States. However, vast parts of the lunar surface are covered with lava. The earliest astronomers mistook these to be water and called them "mare" (Latin for "sea").

Galileo was an unmanned spacecraft sent by NASA to study the planet Jupiter and its moons. The Galileo probe images revealed active volcanoes on Jupiter's moon Io.

Quiet flow

There are no violent volcanic eruptions on the Moon due to the lack of dissolved water and lesser gravity. The lunar mare shows some small volcanic domes and cones, but these are largely flat and comprise broad, slim layers around the vent. Since the Moon's gravity is less than Earth's, the lava is more fluid and flows out easily and quietly over large areas.

The largest volcano on Mars, Olympus Mons, is a circular structure that would span the entire Hawaiian island chain on Earth!

MARS

Largest shield volcanoes

Mars has the largest shield volcanoes in the solar system, though the numbers are few. The "red planet" also has large volcanic cones, marelike volcanic plains and other smaller features. However, there are rarely any active volcanoes on Mars today.

Most numbers

Venus has more volcanoes than any other planet in the solar system. No one can be sure about how many there are, and the total can be even over a million. Most volcanoes on Venus are shield volcanoes, but there are some unusual ones as well. Again, it cannot be proved for certain that the volcanoes are no longer active.

Volcano eruptions on Venus involve fluid lava flows. There is no sign of explosive, ash-forming eruptions.

Famous Volcanoes

There are more than 500 active volcanoes on Earth's surface. These are known to have erupted at least once in recorded history and some of these have gained fame for various reasons.

◀ When Vesuvius erupted in AD 79, the column of ash rose up to nearly 1.2 miles (2 km). The eruption lasted 19 hours, and killed more than 10,000 people.

▼ In 1748, a peasant chanced upon a brick wall, and excavations of Pompeii began. About three-quarters of Pompeii has now been uncovered. Visitors can see buildings as they stood almost 2,000 years ago.

Vesuvius

Mt. Vesuvius is a volcano east of Naples, Italy. One of the most violent explosions on Vesuvius occurred in AD 79, completely destroying the ancient Roman cities of Pompeii and Herculaneum. It has erupted many times since then and is regarded as one of the most dangerous volcanoes in the world.

▲ *The violent eruption of Mount St. Helens in 1980 blew the top of the mountain off, reducing its summit by 1,312 feet (400 m) and replacing it with a horseshoe-shaped crater.*

St. Helens

Mount St. Helens is an active volcano in Washington. The first recorded eruption was in 1800, while the most devastating one took place in 1980. The latter killed 57 people and thousands of animals, and destroyed over 200 homes. The eruption lasted over nine hours.

Mauna Loa

Mauna Loa is the largest active volcano on Earth and makes up nearly half of Hawaii. It is an active shield volcano that erupted last in 1984. In Hawaiian, "mauna loa" means "long mountain."

Mauna Loa is among the most active volcanoes on Earth. It has erupted 33 times since its first recorded eruption in 1843. The most recent one was in 1984.

Mount Etna

Mount Etna is an active volcano on the east coast of Sicily. It is the highest volcano in Europe and has the longest history of recorded eruptions.

More Famous Volcanoes

▼ For generations, Mt. Rainier was known as Takhoma or Tahoma. But on May 8, 1792, Captain George Vancouver of the British Royal Navy officially named it after his friend, Rear Admiral Peter Rainier.

Volcanoes inspire feelings of awe in perhaps everyone. There is more to the phenomenon than just fire and fury, or lava and ash, though. That is the reason why volcanoes have been an object of curiosity and interest among both scientists and common people.

▼ The famous cone-shaped, active Mt. Fuji volcano in Japan remains completely buried in snow in the winter.

Mt. Fuji

Mount Fuji is the highest mountain in Japan. Surrounded by the Five Lakes, it is also one of the most scenic of all volcanoes. The volcano is designated as active, though with low risk of eruption. The last recorded eruption occurred in 1707.

Stromboli

Stromboli has one of the longest recorded periods of activity. It is a small island in the Tyrrhenian Sea, Italy. For at least the last 2,000 years, it has been erupting almost regularly.

Mt. Rainier

Mount Rainier is located in Pierce County, in Washington. Rainier is mostly covered by glaciers. It is a famous destination for winter sports, including snowshoeing and skiing. The most recent eruption was over 175 years ago.

▼ *Kilauea in Hawaii is famed for its frequent eruptions, though most of these are confined within the crater. Some of its major violent explosions were recorded in 1955, 1975 and 1983.*

FACT FILE

- **Mt. Ranier:** Above 14,410 feet (4,392 m)
- **Mt. Fuji:** 12,388 feet (3,776 m)
- **Stromboli:** 2,900 feet (900 m)
- **Kilauea:** 4,009 feet (1,222 m) at the summit

▼ *Lava flow from a volcanic eruption can travel for miles (km) before it cools down and becomes solid. Everything that comes in the way of the hot lava gets knocked down or catches fire. But since the lava flows slowly, people can usually get out of its way in good time.*

Kilauea

Kilauea is one of the world's most active volcanoes, with lava flowing almost continuously. Eruptions at Kilauea happen both from the summit and along the lengthy east and southwest rift zones that extend to the sea.

Volcanology

The study of volcanoes is called volcanology, and the people who study the science are called volcanologists. A volcanologist's job is exciting and adventurous. To become a volcanologist, one needs to study math and science in high school and geology in college.

Predicting eruptions

A volcanologist's main job is to predict volcanic eruptions. Little can be done to stop property damage in the surrounding areas when a volcano explodes. Many lives can be saved, though, if people are shifted to a safe place before the eruption begins.

▲ *The HUGO underwater observatory monitors the Loihi submarine volcano, off Hawaii. The project, begun in 1997, aims to study underwater volcanism.*

◀ *Volcanologists use a special type of thermometer called a thermocouple for measuring the temperature of lava.*

Instruments used

Volcanologists use different instruments to predict an eruption. A tiltmeter is used to measure the expansion of a volcano by estimating the rising or lowering of magma levels. A device called a seismograph helps in detecting earthquakes caused by magma. Thermometers check for temperature rise in the area, while gas detectors measure the quantity of gases.

Geologist measuring the height of a lava fountain at an eruption of the Kīlauea volcano in 1983.

Dangerous mission

Volcanologists must follow strict safety measures since they may be required to work near erupting volcanoes. Observatories have been set up on the slopes or rims of several volcanoes, among them Mount Asama in Japan, Kilauea in Hawaii, and Vesuvius in Italy. The Alaska Observatory keeps track of the 100 active volcanoes in the region.

▲ *The Hawaiian Volcano Observatory (HVO) is perched on the rim of the Kilauea caldera. It was set up in 1912.*

▼ *Volcanologists wear an outfit similar to a spacesuit, along with a helmet and gloves. The suit helps them survive the hot temperature near erupting volcanoes.*

Death on duty

Maurice and Katia Krafft were famous volcanologists who studied and photographed erupting volcanoes all over the world. They were killed by a hot ash flow while photographing the eruption of Unzen in Japan in 1991.

Volcanoes and the Weather

The Earth has witnessed gradual climatic changes over the years. Many factors have led to these changes, and one among them is volcanic eruptions.

▶ Volcanic ash can be ejected to heights of many thousands of feet (m). The gases in the ash can create a haze in the upper layer of the atmosphere and affect global climate patterns.

Small outbursts

Minor eruptions take place around the world on an almost daily basis. In such cases volcanic ash, made up of rock and glass, is spun high into the atmosphere. This has little or no effect on the weather. It is the large eruptions that are likely to have a bigger effect on the climate patterns of the Earth.

Aerosol effect

Volcanic ash is made up of particles and gases including sulphur dioxide. In the high atmosphere, the sulphur dioxide converts into aerosols. These aerosols in turn reflect the Sun's radiation back into outer space, and so less sunlight reaches the Earth's surface. This leads to the cooling of surface temperatures.

◀ When hot lava enters the ocean, white-plume clouds are created by the heat and chemical reactions. These misty clouds are called laze.

◄ When Krakatoa erupted in 1883, the entire northern portion of the island was blown away.

Krakatoa volcano

After the eruption of Krakatoa in Indonesia, in 1883, the volcanic dust was spread around the upper atmosphere by the jet streams. It is believed that world temperatures fell by an estimated 2.2° F (1.2 °C).

INTERESTING FACT

The violent eruption of the Tambora volcano in Indonesia in 1815 led to the pollution of the atmosphere by a large quantity of volcanic dust. In addition to global temperatures falling by 1.8° F (1° C), the following summer turned out to be unusually cold. In fact, the year 1816 came to be termed as "the year without a summer" in parts of Europe and North America.

FACT FILE

KRAKATOA ERUPTION
- ❑ Explosions heard over a third of the Earth's surface
- ❑ Ash thrown up as high as 50 miles (80 km)
- ❑ Extent of material thrown out about 5 cubic miles (21 cu km)

Slowing down

Nonetheless, even the larger volcanic eruptions can only have a short-term effect on the Earth's climate, lasting perhaps a decade or so. Such eruptions will, at the most, only slow down the current trend of global warming rather than permanently halt it.

◄ According to one theory, dinosaurs disappeared from the Earth due to volcanic eruptions. Over a period of several million years, volcanoes could have created enough dust and soot to block out sunlight. As a result, food became scarce and temperatures changed. Some scientists believe dinosaurs could not adapt and died out.

Earthquakes

Various disturbances beneath the Earth's surface cause the ground to jolt or shake. This is called an earthquake. A strong earthquake can rattle many things, including buildings and bridges.

Faulty lines

Most earthquakes occur along a fault, which is a line or lines of fracture between blocks of rocks on the Earth's crust. As the tectonic plates move, they collide, move apart, or slide past one another, often causing faults. The presence of faults allows the rocks to shift relative to each other—one of the major factors behind earthquakes.

▼ *The San Andreas Fault in California is the point where the Pacific Plate and the North American Plate move against each other.*

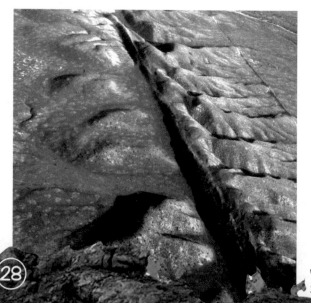

High stress

Over a period of time, built-up stress within the Earth causes large blocks of rock along a fault to strain, or bend. When the stress becomes too much, the resultant sudden release of energy by the rocks causes an earthquake.

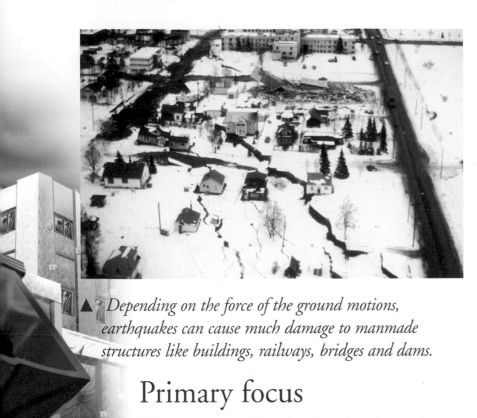

▲ *Depending on the force of the ground motions, earthquakes can cause much damage to manmade structures like buildings, railways, bridges and dams.*

Primary focus

The point within the Earth where the rocks first break or shift is called the focus or hypocenter of the quake. The focus of most earthquakes lies within 43 miles (70 km) beneath the surface, though the deepest can be at 435 miles (700 km).

Hypocenter

Epicenter

Seismic waves

Fault line

Epicenter

The point on the Earth's surface directly above the focus is the epicenter of the quake. The strongest shaking is usually felt near the epicenter.

◄ *The focus is the point of sudden movement inside the Earth wherein an earthquake occurs. The shock waves then travel towards the ground surface.*

Famous Earthquakes

Earthquakes almost never kill people directly. Rather, the deaths and injuries are caused due to the collapse of manmade structures like buildings, bridges and houses, or by fires resulting from broken gas and water lines. There is also danger from rockfalls and falling trees or tree branches.

Fire hazard

A major cause of death and property damage in earthquakes is fire. The 1906 San Francisco earthquake ranks as one of the worst disasters in American history because of a fire that raged for three days in the aftermath.

▲ *The California earthquake of April 18, 1906, lasted about 45 to 60 seconds, killing over 700 people.*

Chilean quake

The Great Chilean Earthquake of May 22, 1960, is the largest earthquake in recorded history. The earthquake originated along the southern Chilean coast and caused a tsunami that hit Hawaii and the coastal areas of South America. About 3,000 people were killed in the earthquake/tsunami.

◀ *More than 90 percent of the deaths during the 1964 earthquake in Alaska were due to the tsunamis that hit the coast after the shocks.*

▲ *The Great Kanto Earthquake, which shook Tokyo and Yokohama in Japan in 1923, left a trail of destructive fires.*

Japan hit

The Great Kanto Earthquake in Japan, on September 1, 1923, caused huge destruction. Over one hundred thousand people were killed in the quake, which had a magnitude of 7.9 on the Richter scale. More than 88 fires broke out due to the quake.

▲ *The earthquake that struck San Fernando on February 9, 1971, ranks as one of the worst in the history of California. Measuring 6.5 on the Richter scale, the calamity caused the deaths of over 60 persons and extensive property damage.*

Most deadly

The world's deadliest earthquake on record occurred in central China in 1556. Most people in the region lived in caves carved from soft rock. As the caves started to collapse during the earthquake, an estimated 830,000 people lost their lives.

Measuring Earthquakes

While an earthquake cannot be predicted accurately, scientists can measure its intensity. They can also accurately pinpoint the epicenter and hypocenter of the earthquake.

Richter scale

The most common instrument for measuring earthquake intensity is the Richter scale. It was developed in 1935 by seismologists Beno Gutenberg of Germany and Charles F. Richter of the United States. The scale is a series of numbers from 1 to 10, and each increase in number means an increase by a power of 10.

▲ *Chinese philosopher Chang Hêng invented the earliest known seismoscope in AD 132. It resembled a wine jar with a 6-foot (1.8 m) diameter. On the outside it had eight dragon heads facing the eight principal directions of the compass. During an earthquake, one of the dragon mouths would release a ball, depending on the direction of the shaking.*

Increasing intensity

Every increase of one number in magnitude means the energy release of the quake is 32 times greater. For example, an earthquake of magnitude 7.0 releases 32 times more energy than an earthquake measuring 6.0.

◄ *About 80 percent of the world's major earthquakes happen along a belt encircling the Pacific Ocean, called the Ring of Fire.*

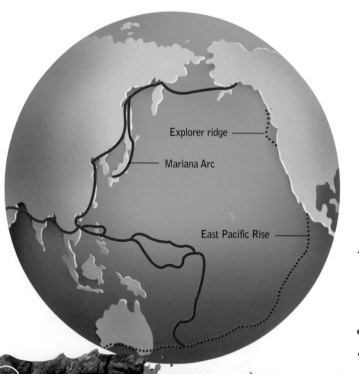

Explorer ridge

Mariana Arc

East Pacific Rise

———— Mid-ocean ridge system

·············· Island arc/Trench systems

Seismic measure

The strength and location of earthquakes are recorded using an instrument known as a seismograph. It has sensors called seismometers that can detect movements in the ground.

▼ *The instruments at Honolulu geophysical observatory monitor tidal levels at remote sites throughout the Pacific Basin. These are used to warn about tsunamis.*

Surface wave

First P wave

First S wave

1 minute

◀ *Scientists use the geodimeter to monitor changes on the Earth's surface near faults over a period of time. Thereby they hope to predict an earthquake with more accuracy.*

▲ *The zigzag line made by a seismograph is called a seismogram. It shows the changing intensity of the vibrations from an earthquake.*

Predictions

Scientists make long-term predictions of where earthquakes can occur. However, they are yet to develop a method to predict the exact time of an earthquake.

Features of Volcanoes and Earthquakes

▼ Earthquakes can trigger landslides that cause loss of life and great damage to property.

Some earthquakes are caused by the movement of magma in volcanoes, and such quakes can be an early warning of volcanic eruptions. Earthquakes and volcanoes also give rise to phenomena like tsunamis, mudflows, ash flows and landslides.

Flow of mud

Mudflows usually originate in volcanoes with large masses of ice and snow on their summits. They are caused by the speedy melting of a large amount of ice, caused by a volcanic eruption or due to an ice avalanche that has broken free because of an earthquake. These fast moving streams of mud sweep away anything in their path.

Tsunami crashes

Large earthquakes, and occasionally volcanic eruptions, beneath the ocean can create a series of huge, destructive waves called tsunamis that flood the coasts. Tsunamis gain in height when they reach shallow water near the shore.

◄ Sometimes, volcanic ash combines with water in a stream and forms a boiling mudflow, which can be highly destructive.

► *Before the tsunami hits the coast, the sea often recedes from the coast, like it did at the Kalutara Beach in Sri Lanka in 2004. If the slope is shallow, the withdrawal can exceed 2,625 feet (800 m).*

Indian Ocean

On December 26, 2004, an earthquake of magnitude 9.0 in the Indian Ocean triggered a series of killer tsunamis. At least 160,000 people were killed, making it the deadliest tsunami in recorded history.

Caught unawares

People who are unaware of the danger that accompanies a tsunami may often remain at the shore due to curiosity, or perhaps to collect fish when the sea withdraws before a tsunami. And when the tsunami strikes with all its force, it is often too late for them to run.

► *The tsunamis of 2004 caused widespread destruction in Aceh in Indonesia. This picture shows a calm coastline before December 26, 2004.*

► *The tsunamis that struck the Indian Ocean in 2004 washed away everything in their way—roads, buildings, bridges and hundreds of thousands of people.*

In Preparation

Earthquakes can strike any time, and foolproof warning systems are yet to be developed, so we must look to special building techniques and survival knowledge to protect ourselves.

◀ *The suspension bridge across the Tagus River in Lisbon, Portugal, was designed to withstand major earthquakes. One of its foundations was secured 260 feet (79 m) deep under the water.*

Building structures

Special building techniques in earthquake-prone areas can help reduce injury, loss of life, and property damage when disaster does strike. Earthquake-resistant techniques include bolting buildings to their foundations and erecting support walls called shear walls.

▶ *The Beehive Parliament House in New Zealand is just 1,312 feet (400 m) from the Wellington fault zone, which is capable of causing big earthquakes. The building had to be rebuilt with new foundations, stronger walls and new beams. Specially made blocks of rubber and lead were placed between the foundations and the main beams.*

Fastened down

In earthquake-resistant homes, schools and workplaces, structures such as heavy appliances and furniture are fastened down to prevent them from falling over when the building shakes. Gas and water lines are purposely laid with flexible joints to prevent leakage.

FACT FILE

LARGEST EVACUATIONS DUE TO EARTHQUAKES THAT CAUSED VOLCANIC ERUPTIONS
- **Nyiragongo, 2002:** About 500,000 evacuated in Congo
- **Pinatubo, 1991:** About 250,000 evacuated in the Philippines
- **Galunggung, 1982:** About 75,000 evacuated in Indonesia
- **Mayon, 1984:** About 73,000 evacuated in the Philippines

If stuck indoors during an earthquake, the best safety measure is to take cover under a piece of heavy furniture and hold on to it, or simply stand against an inside wall.

The aftershocks

A large earthquake may be accompanied by many quakes of smaller magnitude. These later quakes are called aftershocks and can cause immense damage. The safe option is to steer clear of walls, windows, staircases and smashed structures that could crash.

Evacuation

Unlike earthquakes, a volcano eruption can be predicted more certainly. Once volcanologists warn of an eruption, the area around the volcano is evacuated. While damage to property cannot be avoided, lives can definitely be saved.

Rescue Mission

Relief and rescue efforts must be put in operation immediately after the disaster strikes. Rescue workers look for survivors in the aftermath of an earthquake or a volcanic eruption.

Honeycombed in

Collapsed buildings are like honeycombs with empty spaces, which allow those trapped inside to survive. In the instance of the 1992 Philippines earthquake, a man was extracted with a broken ankle after 13 days trapped in a hotel that had collapsed during the event.

▼ *A rescue team waits for a building to be propped up, before entering. Buildings weakened by earthquakes can collapse well after the shock.*

Miracles

Often, unusual survival stories are termed as "miracles". The rescue team, however, knows that such a possibility always exists. It has to be careful and patient while digging through the rubble.

▼ *People trapped in earthquake rubble stand a better chance of survival if they are rescued within 72 hours.*

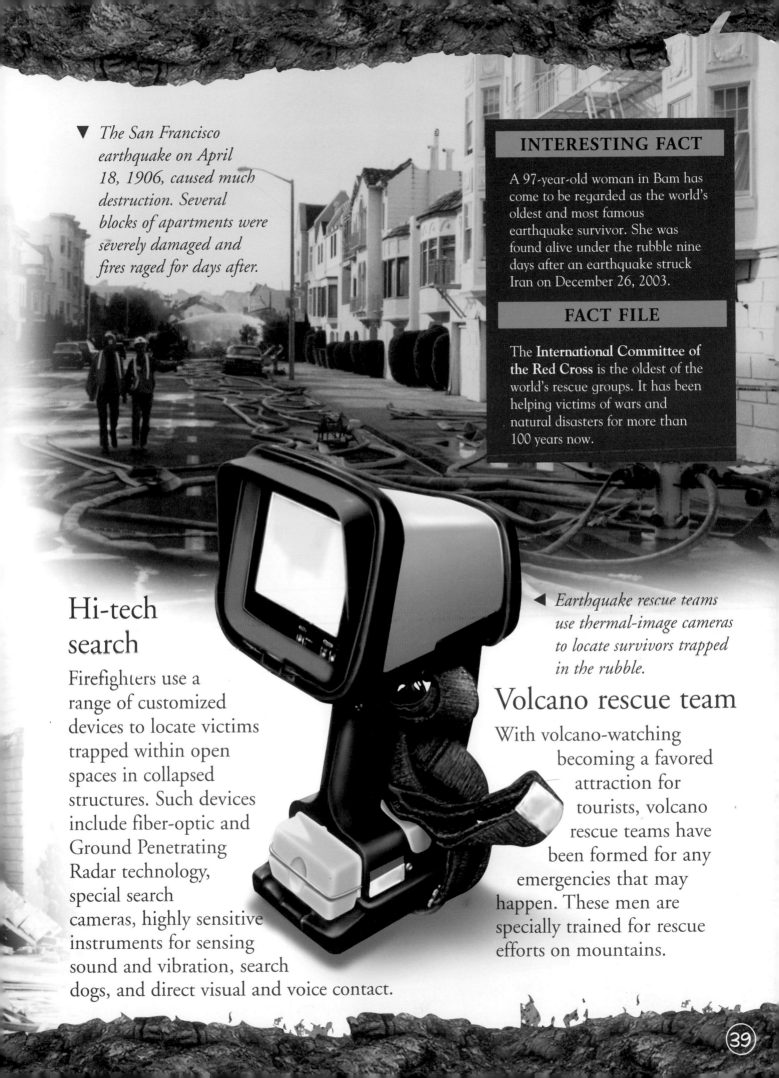

▼ *The San Francisco earthquake on April 18, 1906, caused much destruction. Several blocks of apartments were severely damaged and fires raged for days after.*

Hi-tech search

Firefighters use a range of customized devices to locate victims trapped within open spaces in collapsed structures. Such devices include fiber-optic and Ground Penetrating Radar technology, special search cameras, highly sensitive instruments for sensing sound and vibration, search dogs, and direct visual and voice contact.

◀ *Earthquake rescue teams use thermal-image cameras to locate survivors trapped in the rubble.*

Volcano rescue team

With volcano-watching becoming a favored attraction for tourists, volcano rescue teams have been formed for any emergencies that may happen. These men are specially trained for rescue efforts on mountains.

Legends

Around the world, various people have tried to explain earthquakes and volcanoes in different ways. Here are some legends about what makes the ground shake and erupt!

Devilish moves

In Mexico, it was believed that El Diablo, the devil, made giant cuts in the Earth from the inside. Thus, he and his devilish friends could use the cracks to go up and carry out mischief on Earth whenever they wanted to.

According to Mexican legend, earthquakes are caused when the devil makes giant rips in the Earth from the inside!

Vulcan's forge

People in Sicily believed that the lava fragments and dust clouds erupting from a volcano came from the god Vulcan's forge as he cut out thunderbolts for Jupiter, king of the gods, and weapons for Mars, the god of war. Vulcan was the god of fire in Roman religion.

The word "volcano" comes from the island of Vulcano, off Sicily. Centuries ago, people there believed that Vulcano was the chimney of the god Vulcan's forge

Baby Ru

A legend in New Zealand has it that Mother Earth carries within her womb a child, the young god Ru. And every time he stretches and kicks, an earthquake happens!

◀ *Hawaiian people attributed volcanic activity to the beautiful but wrathful Pele, the goddess of fire. Whenever she was angry or spiteful, she made volcanoes erupt with fire!*

◀ *In the fourth century BC, Aristotle proposed that earthquakes were caused by winds trapped in caves under the ground.*

Greek idea

In Greece, the philosopher Aristotle proposed that strong, unruly winds are trapped in underground caverns. As these winds thrash about struggling to escape, earthquakes hit the Earth.

Fascinating Facts

Volcanoes are nature's fireworks on display, while earthquakes occur when the Earth gets a bit shaken up. While both cause large-scale damage, they are nonetheless very fascinating. In fact, tourists are known to throng to volcanic areas in hopes of catching a glimpse of streaming lava or surging smoke.

Close quarters

Volcanologists have ventured into the craters of some volcanoes. Nobody has gone all the way down, though, since it is too hot and filled with poisonous gases. One can only learn about the way volcanoes work by looking down old craters.

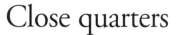

▼ *Volcanologists have to sometimes explore inside a crater to collect rock and gas samples for study.*

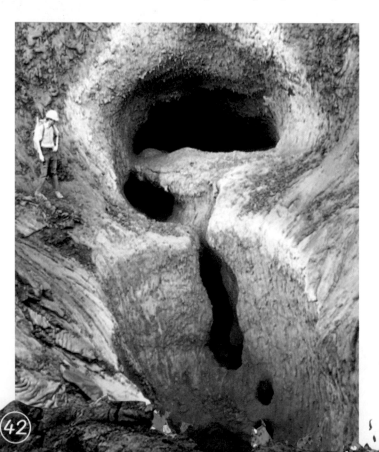

Moonquakes

Moonquakes (tremors on the Moon's surface) have been observed to occur, but their frequency is less than that of earthquakes. Also, moonquakes are much smaller in magnitude than the quakes on Earth. Most moonquakes occur at great depth, about halfway between the surface and the center of the Moon.

▶ *Moonquakes were first discovered during the Apollo missions to the Moon. Moonquakes are much weaker than earthquakes, as the Moon's core is colder and has a solid mantle, unlike the Earth's molten mantle.*

◀ *Alaska is one of the most earthquake-prone areas in the world, with over 4,000 earthquakes recorded at various depths in a year.*

The animal sense

It is believed that animals can sense the onset of earthquakes, and that they start behaving strangely. Such changes in behavior cannot, however, be used to predict earthquakes precisely, since a connection between a specific behavior and the occurrence of an earthquake has not been made yet.

▶ *It is believed that animals can sense earthquakes beforehand. In 373 BC, for instance, rats, snakes and weasels deserted the Greek city of Helice in droves just days before a devastating earthquake struck.*

Manmade quakes

Human beings have also been responsible for causing earthquakes. The building-up of large masses of water behind dams, digging of mines, injection of fluid into the Earth's crust, and detonation of huge bombs are some human activities that can lead to earthquakes.

Glossary

Aerosol (ER-uh-sahl) Fine liquid or gas particles that are distributed through gas, usually air

Avalanche (A-vuh-lanch) Large mass of rock debris or snow that slides down a mountain slope rapidly and forcefully

Basalt (buh-SOLT) Volcanic rock that is dark in color and usually dense and smooth

Black sand (BLAK SAND) Created by the interaction of hot lava with cold seawater, as a result of which the lava bubble bursts to form small crystals

Climate change (KLY-mut CHAYNJ) Long-term, major change recorded in the weather trends of an area

Conduit (KAHN-doo-ut) Channel that conveys water or other fluid

Core (KOR) The extremely hot center of the Earth, existing in a largely molten state; composed of a large quantity of iron

Debris (deh-BREE) Collection of fragments of rock and other material

Detonation (deh-tun-AY-shun) An explosion, or the act of exploding

Evacuation (ih-va-kyuh-WAY-shun) Shifting from a place of danger to one of greater safety

Fatality (fay-TA-luh-tee) Death brought on by an accident or a disaster

Fumarole (FYOO-muh-rohl) Volcanic vent that issues forth gas and steam

Geologist (jee-AH-luh-jist) Scientist who studies the origin, history, structure and composition of the Earth

Granite (GRA-nut) Light-colored, coarse igneous rock; formed by the cooling of magma under the Earth's crust

Gravity (GRA-vuh-tee) The force of attraction that pulls bodies toward the center of a celestial body, such as the Earth

Hotspot (HAHT-spaht) Region inside the Earth marked by extreme heat and believed to be the site of active volcanic activity

Igneous rock (IG-nee-us RAHK) Formed when magma cools down and becomes solid

Landslide (LAND-slyd) Downward movement of a mass of rock or earth, along a slope

Lava (LAH-vuh) Molten rock (magma) that reaches the Earth's surface

Lunar (LOO-nur) Relating to the Earth's Moon

Magma (MAG-muh) Molten or partially molten rock found under the Earth's crust

Magma chamber (MAG-muh CHAYM-ber) Underground reservoir, especially beneath a volcano, holding molten material

Magnitude (MAG-nuh-tood) Measure of the amount of energy released during an earthquake; recorded on the Richter scale

Mid-ocean ridge
(MID-oh-shun RIJ) Series of mountain ranges along the ocean basin

NASA (NA-suh) National Aeronautics and Space Administration, an independent agency of the United States government for space research

Observatory
(ub-ZER-vuh-tor-ee) A place equipped for studying astronomical, weather-related or other natural phenomena

Pillow lava (PIH-loh LAH-vuh) Volcanic lava hardened into an elongated, pillow-shaped formation; formed underwater

Pumice (PUH-mus) Light, frothy volcanic rock formed from rapidly cooling lava that is full of gas

Pyroclastic (py-roh-KLAS-tik) Rock or mineral fragment formed during a volcanic eruption

Radiation (ray-dee-AY-shun) Emission and transmission of energy in the form of rays and waves

Rheumatism
(ROO-muh-tih-zum) A variety of disorders of the muscles, joints or connective tissue

Seismic wave (SYZ-mik WAYV) Vibration caused by an earthquake or explosion inside the Earth

Seismogram (SYZ-muh-gram) Diagram of earthquake waves recorded by a seismograph

Seismograph (SYZ-muh-graf) Instrument that records earthquake waves

Stress (STRES) The resisting force built up in a body due to an external force

Submarine (SUB-muh-reen) Below the surface of the sea

Tephra (TEH-fruh) Solid matter ejected into the air during a volcanic eruption

Tidal wave (TY-dul WAYV) A large wave along the seashore often caused by wind and high tide

Tiltmeter (TILT-mee-ter) Instrument to measure the expansion of a volcano by tracking the rising or lowering of magma levels

Toxic (TAHK-sik) Capable of causing health problem or even death, particularly by chemicals

Tsunami (tsu-NAH-mee) Very large ocean wave usually caused by an underwater earthquake, and occasionally by submarine landslides and volcanic eruptions

Further Reading & Web Sites

Hunter, Rebecca. *Volcanoes and Earthquakes*. Chicago: Raintree, 2004.

Rooney, Anne. *Explore It: Earthquakes and Volcanoes*. Berkeley, CA: Silver Dolphin Books, 2006.

Townsend, John. *Earthquakes and Volcanoes—a Survival Guide: Earth's Physical Processes*. Chicago: Raintree, 2005.

Volcanoes and Earthquakes. New York: DK Children, 2004.

Due to the changing nature of Internet links, PowerKids Press has developed an online list of Web sites related to the subject of this book. This site is updated regularly. Please use this link to access the list:
www.powerkidslinks.com/wnat/volcano/

Index

Index